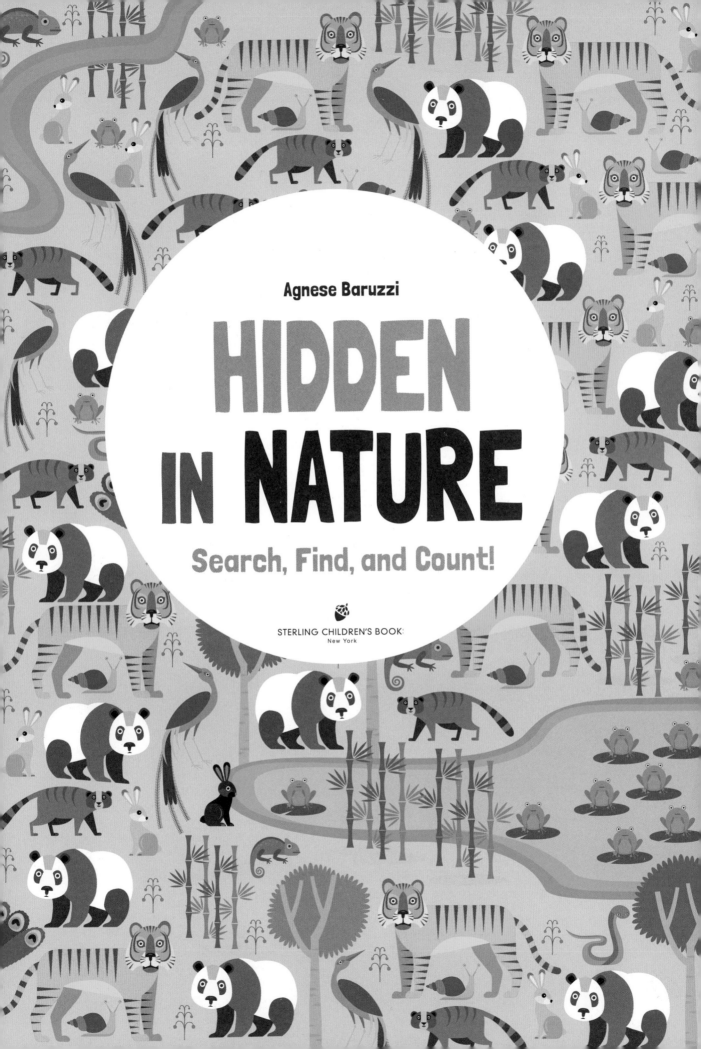

Agnese Baruzzi

HIDDEN IN NATURE

Search, Find, and Count!

STERLING CHILDREN'S BOOKS
New York

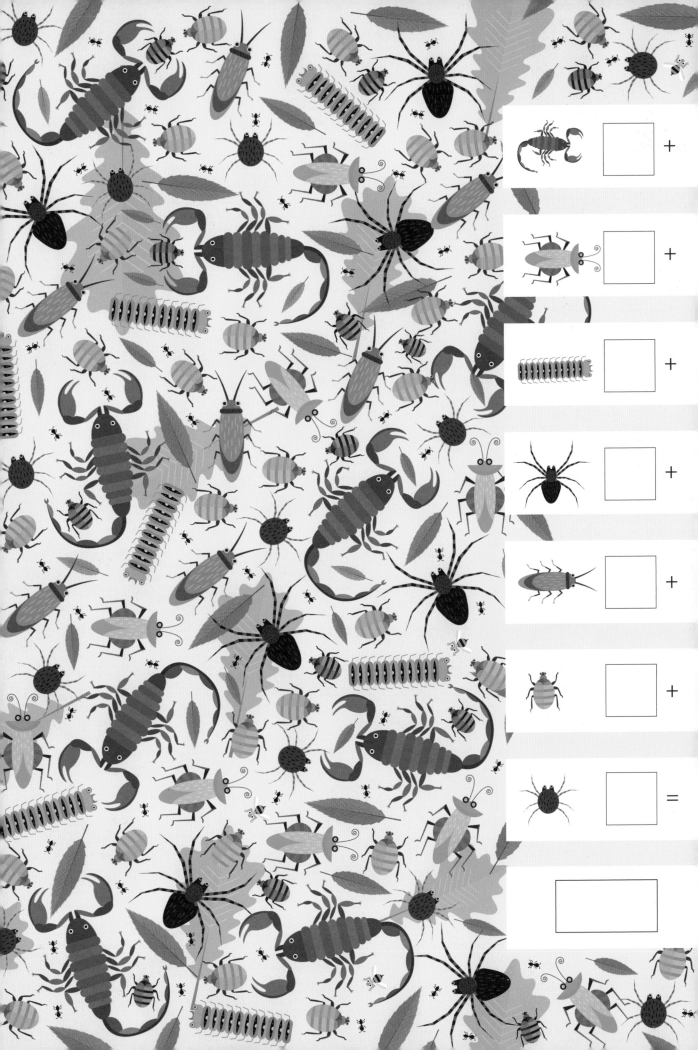

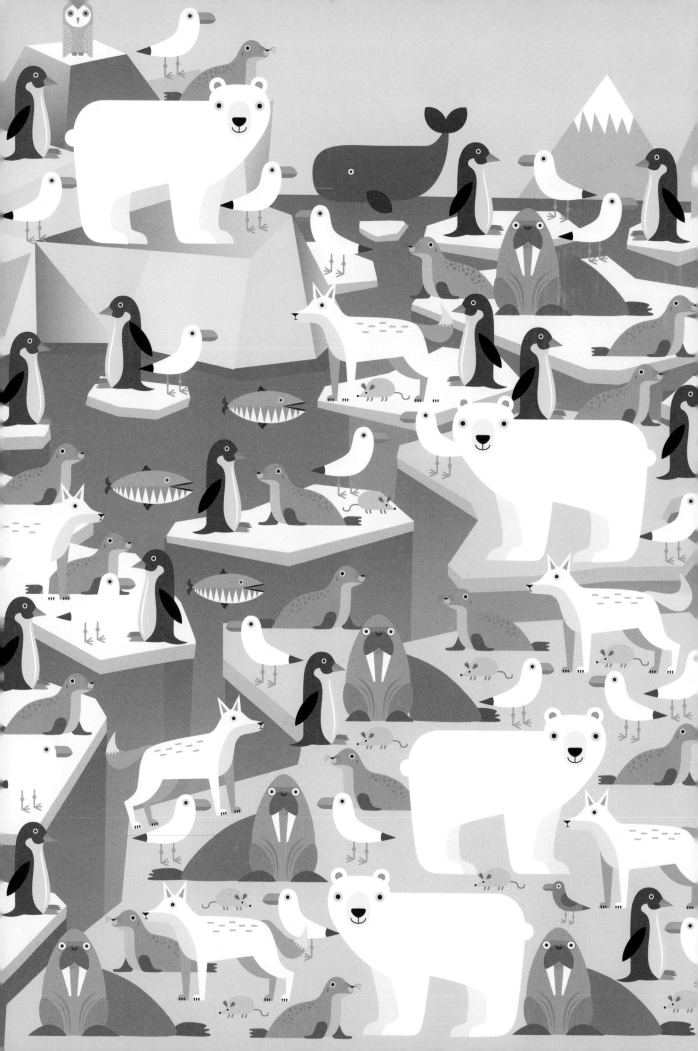

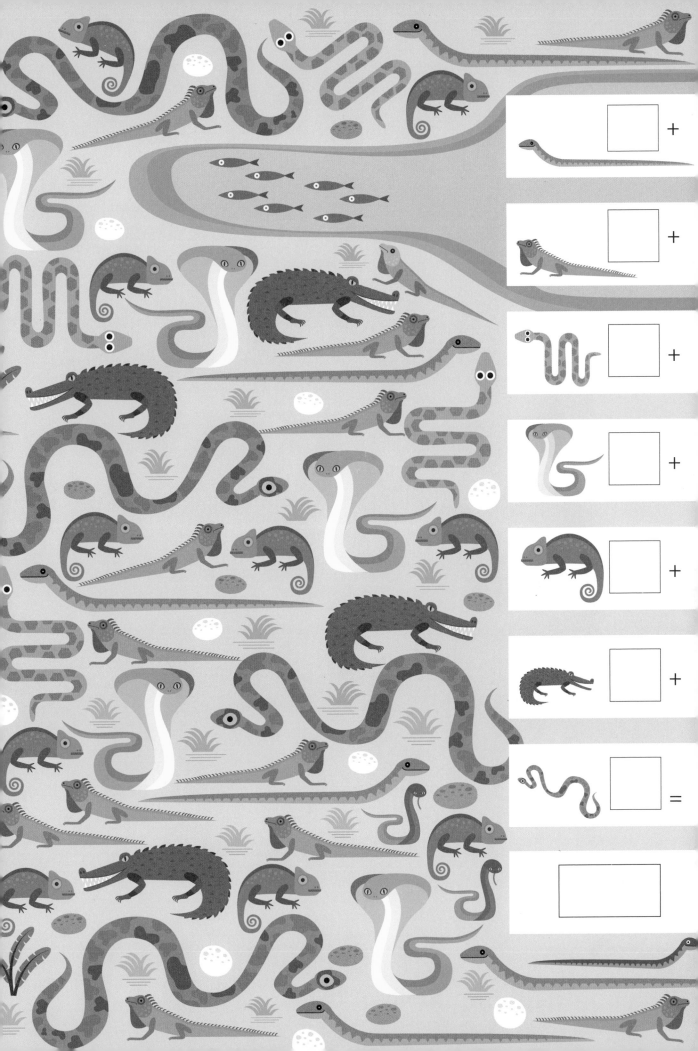

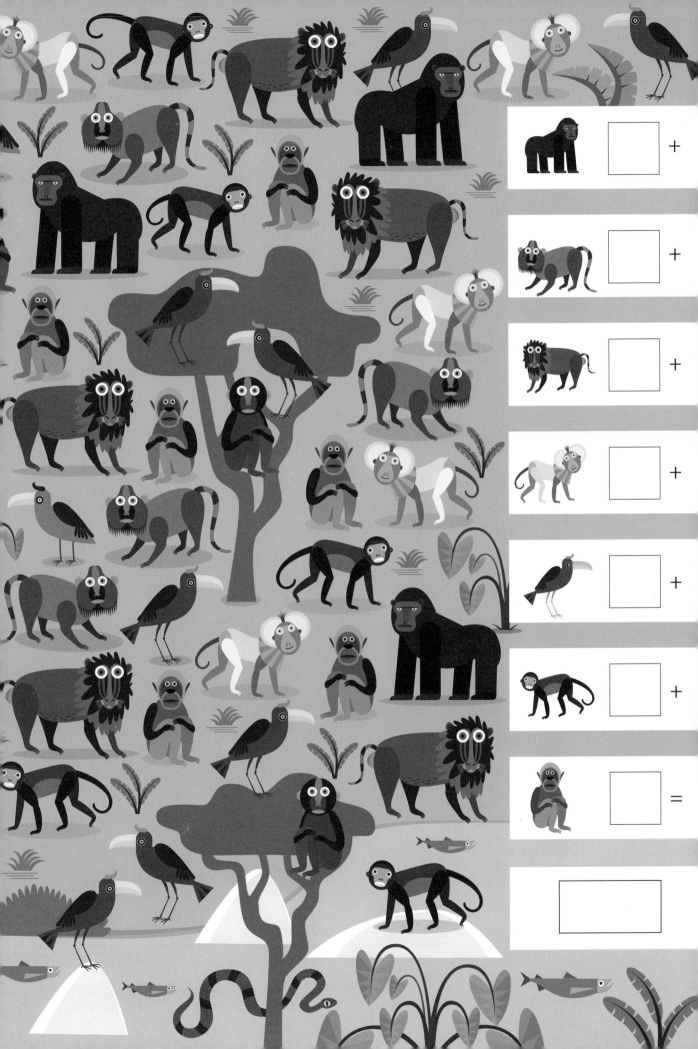

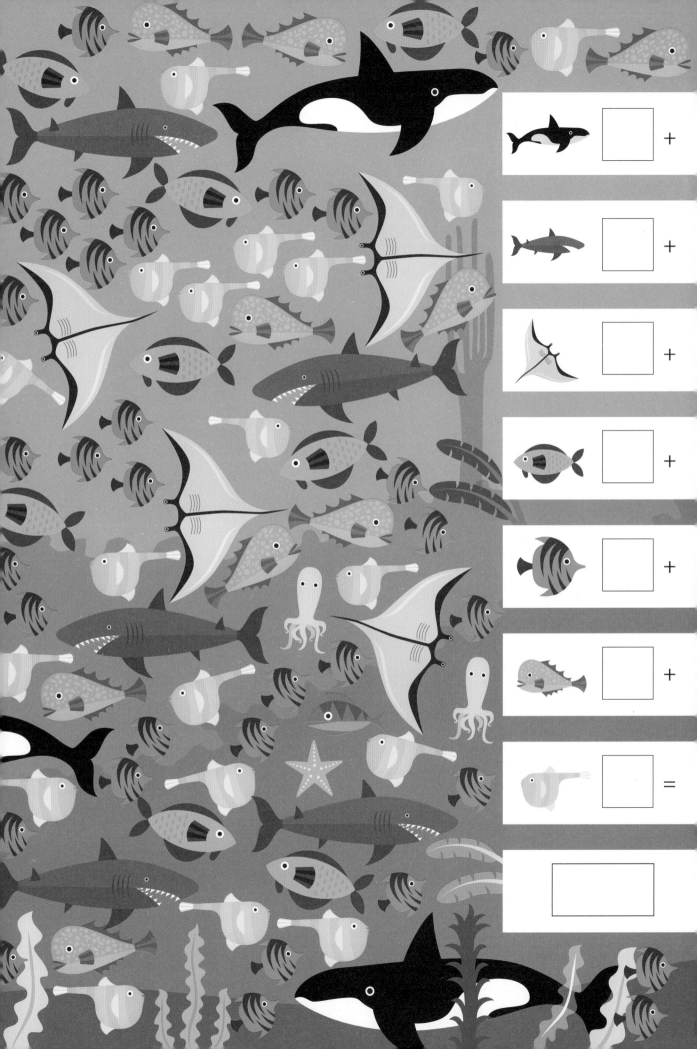

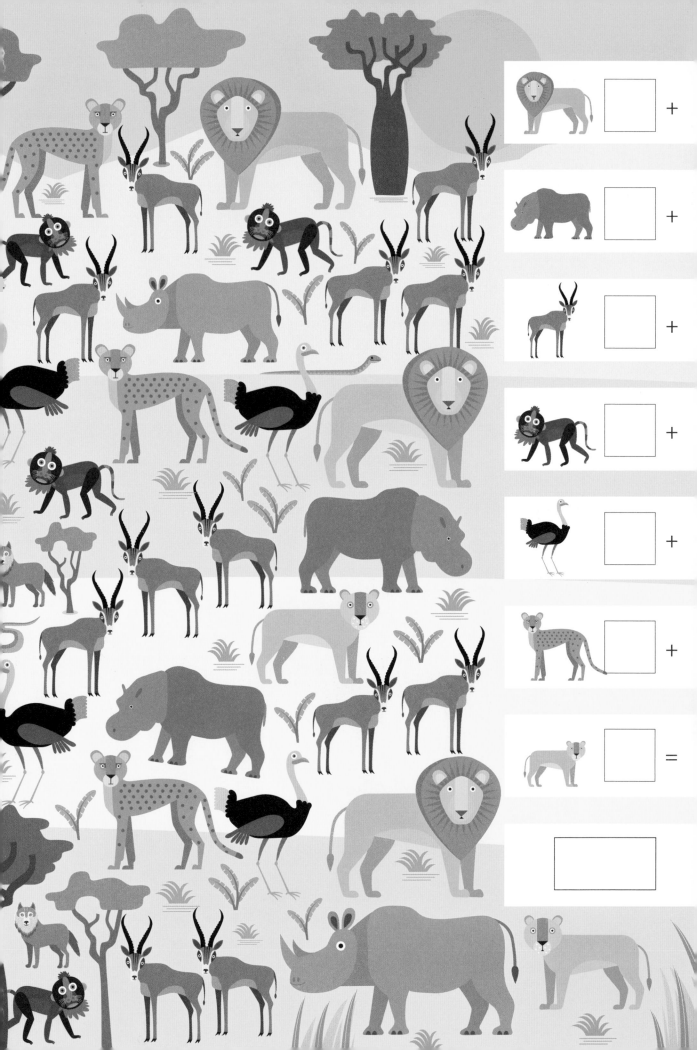

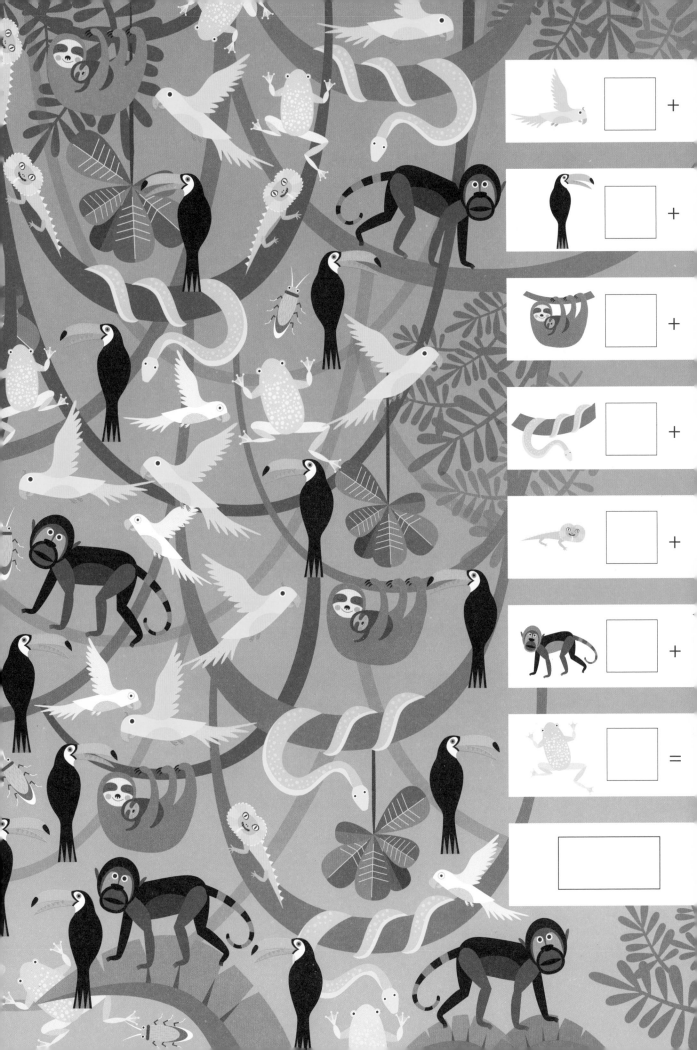

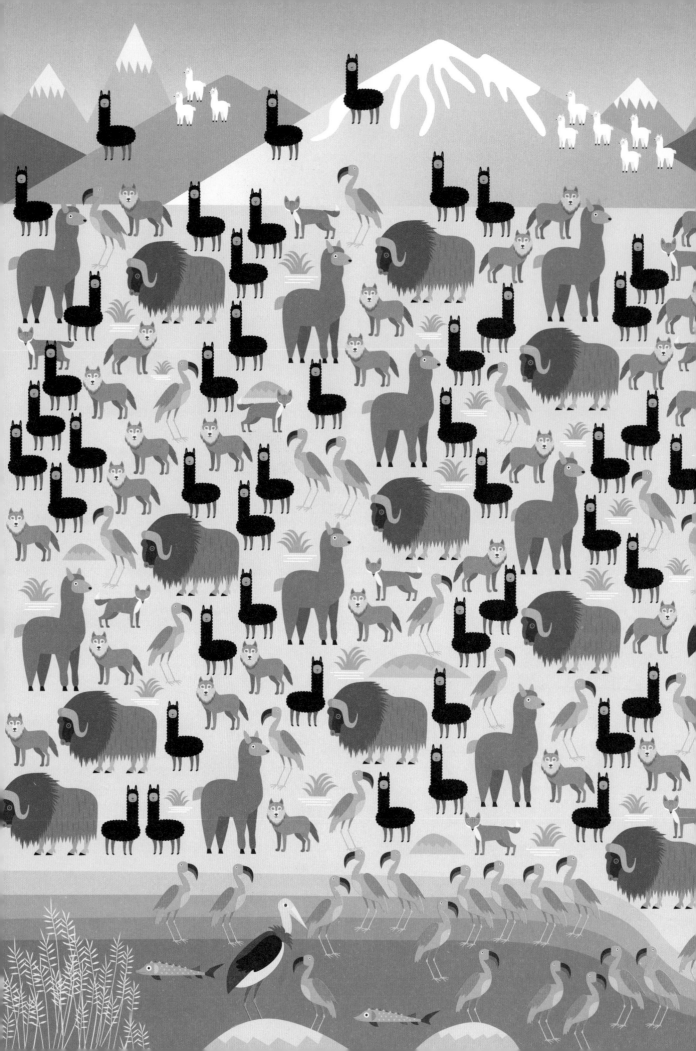

Have you found ALL OF THEM?

CHECK YOUR ANSWERS HERE

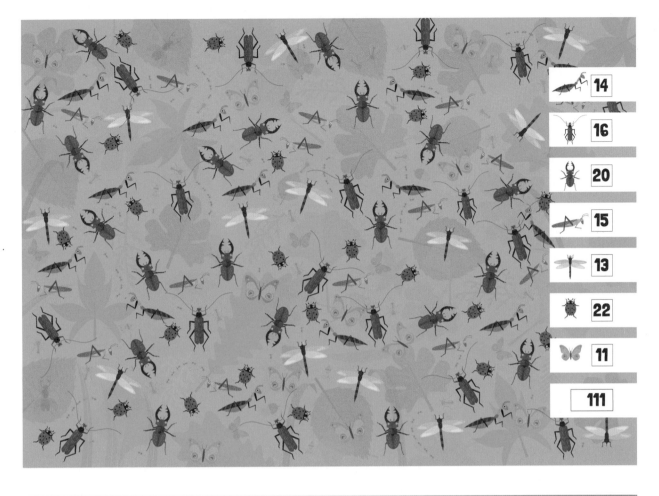

14
16
20
15
13
22
11
111

6
10
10
17
8
7
12
70

	47
	15
	33
	25
	26
	12
	13
	5
	176

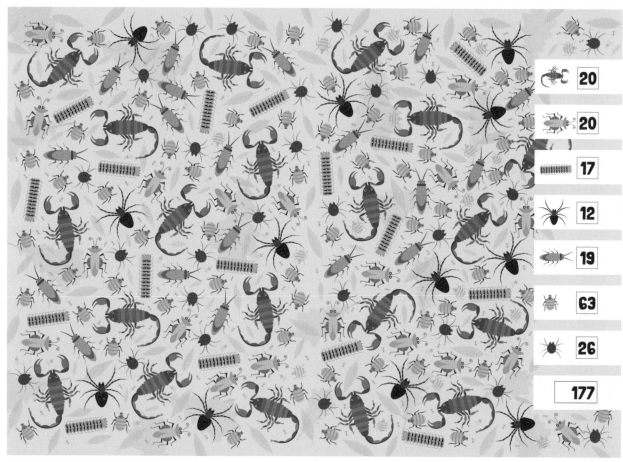

	20
	20
	17
	12
	19
	63
	26
	177

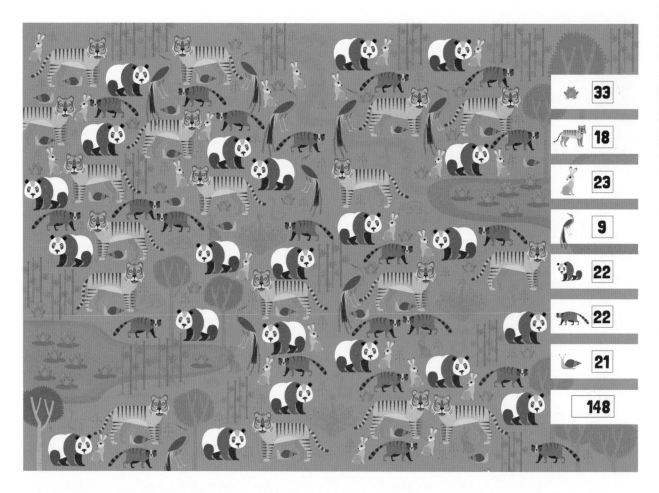

🍁	33
🐯	18
🐰	23
🦚	9
🐼	22
🦝	22
🐌	21
148	

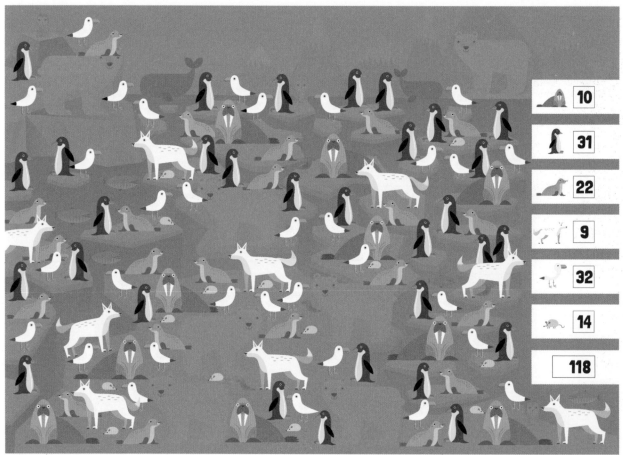

🦭	10
🐧	31
🦭	22
🦊	9
🕊️	32
🐭	14
118	

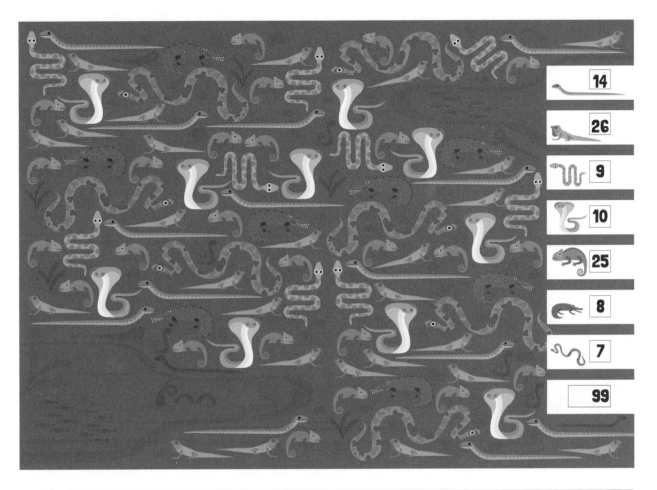

14

26

9

10

25

8

7

99

10

12

10

13

19

11

16

91

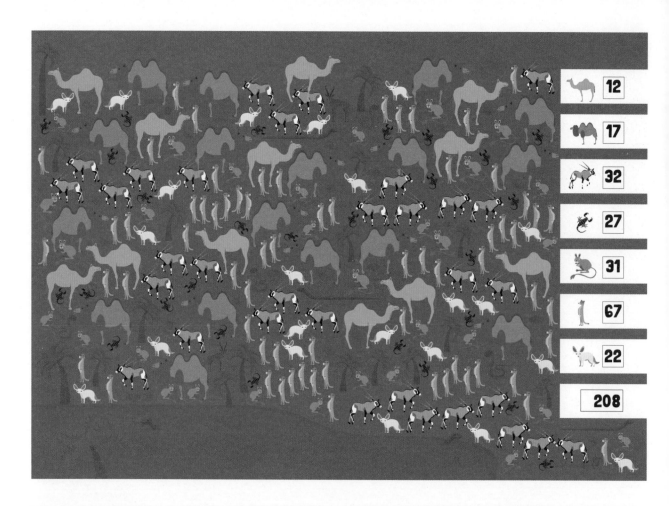

🐫	12
🐫	17
🦌	32
🦂	27
🐀	31
🦝	67
🦊	22
	208

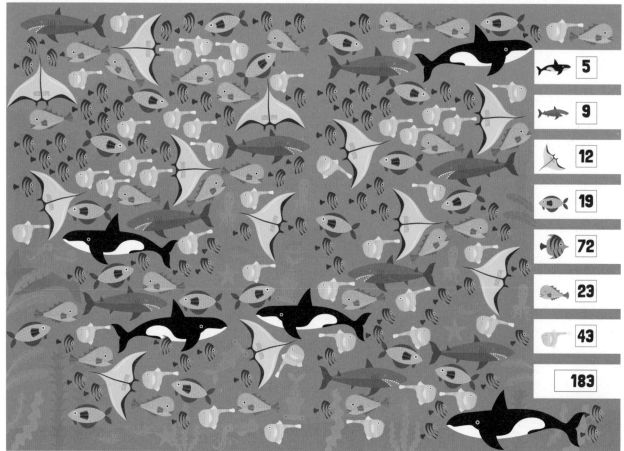

🐋	5
🦈	9
🐟	12
🐟	19
🐠	72
🐡	23
🐚	43
	183

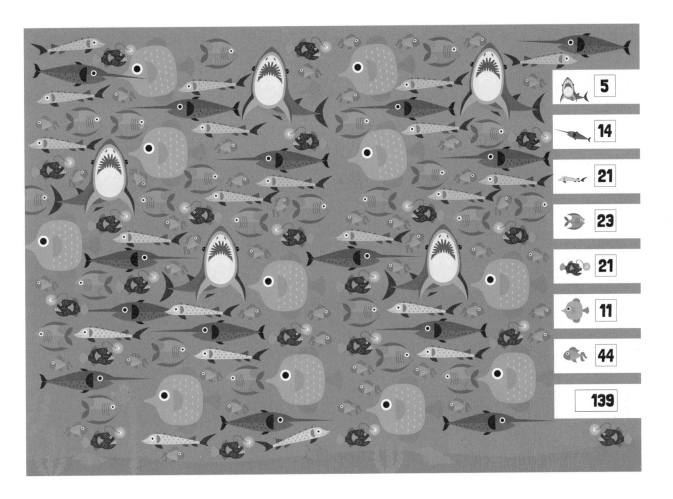

shark	5
swordfish	14
needlefish	21
angelfish	23
anglerfish	21
pufferfish	11
clownfish	44
139	

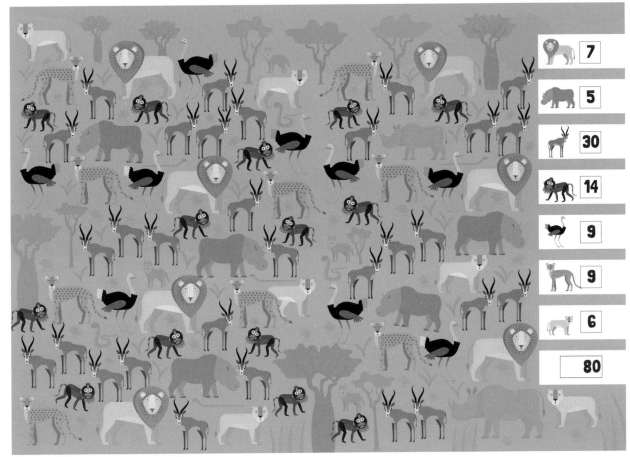

lion	7
rhino	5
gazelle	30
baboon	14
ostrich	9
cheetah	9
lioness	6
80	

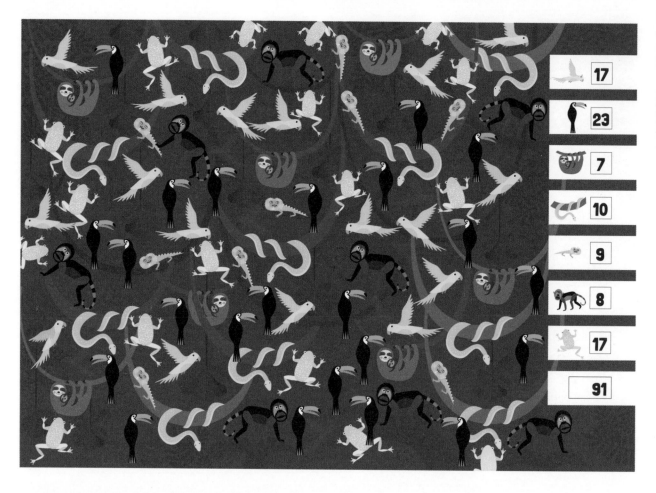

🦜	**17**
🦤	**23**
🦥	**7**
🐍	**10**
🦎	**9**
🐒	**8**
🐸	**17**
	91

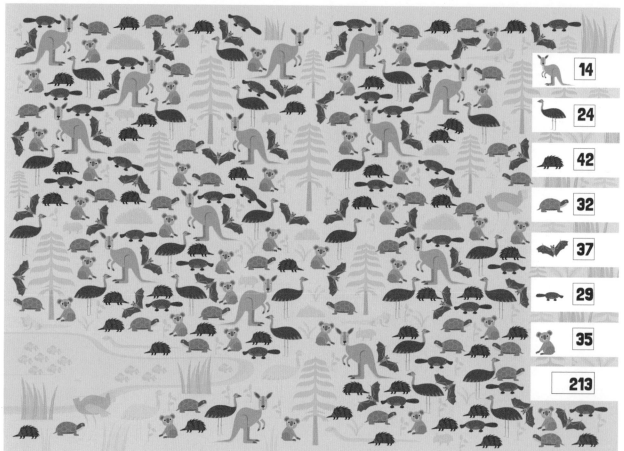

🦘	**14**
🦤	**24**
🦔	**42**
🐢	**32**
🦇	**37**
🦫	**29**
🐨	**35**
	213

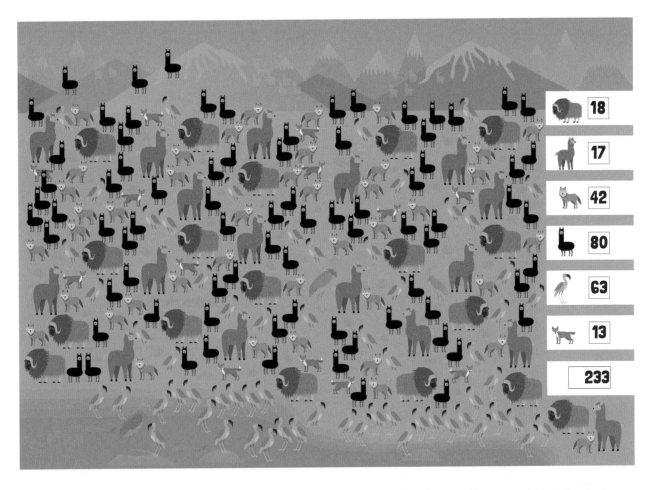

18
17
42
80
63
13
233

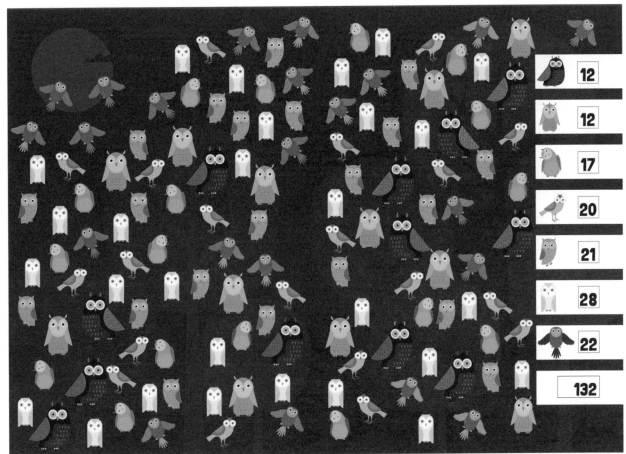

12
12
17
20
21
28
22
132

STERLING CHILDREN'S BOOKS
New York

An Imprint of Sterling Publishing Co., Inc.
1166 Avenue of the Americas
New York, NY 10036

© 2017 White Star s.r.l.

First Sterling edition published in 2018.

ISBN 978-1-4549-2937-6

Distributed in Canada by Sterling Publishing
c/o Canadian Manda Group, 664 Annette Street
Toronto, Ontario, M6S 2C8, Canada

For information about custom editions, special sales, and premium and corporate
purchases, please contact Sterling Special Sales at 800-805-5489 or specialsales@
sterlingpublishing.com.

Manufactured in China
Lot #:
2 4 6 8 10 9 7 5 3 1
11/17

sterlingpublishing.com